They're here!

Richard Harland

Ginn is an imprint of Pearson education Limited, a company incorporated in England and Wales, having its registered office at Edinburgh Gate, Harlow, Essex, CM20 2JE. Registered company number: 872828

Visit www.ginn.co.uk to see a chart showing you all the Pocket Reads programme information you will need.

They're Here! © Richard Harland 2002

From the Spinouts project developed by Paul Collins and Meredith Costain.

This book is copyright and reproduction of the whole or part without the publisher's written permission is prohibited.

09
10 9 8 7 6 5
ISBN 978 0 602242 74 9

Illustrated by Phil Garner and Mitch Vane
Cover illustration by Marc McBride
Designed by Carolyn Gibson
Repro by Digital Imaging, Glasgow
Printed and bound in China (GCC/05)

Richard Harland

Richard Harland is a full-time writer who lives in New South Wales, Australia. He has written several science fiction and fantasy novels for young people.

About the story

"Kristy O'Connell first appeared in another story I wrote. So naturally she wanted to get into this story too. How could I stop her? She'll do just about anything to be a megastar!"

CHAPTER 1

Run For Your Life!

"Dad! Quick! Dad!"

Kristy's dad was coming in through the front gate. She rushed up to him. Her eyes were wide and she was trembling all over.

"What is it, Kristy?" asked Dad. "What's the matter, pet?"

Kristy grabbed Dad's arm. "You won't believe it! I can't describe it!"

Kristy pulled Dad through the front garden and round the side of the house.

"It's horrible! So scary! You won't be scared, will you?"

"Of course not," said Dad.

He followed Kristy across the back lawn. Beyond the lawn was the garden shed and a field with lots of bushes. She led him along the path between the bushes.

"It was there!" She pointed at a thick clump of bushes. "Where's it gone?"

There was nothing there now. Dad turned and held Kristy gently by the shoulders.

"Calm down and tell me what you saw," he said.

"It was yellow!" Kristy said. "And slimy! It had hundreds of eyes!"

"Kristy, Kristy," said Dad. "You've been watching too much TV. You –"

Kristy screamed. She was staring at something right behind Dad.

Dad spun around and stared.

It was a huge yellow creature rising above the bushes. Its skin was slimy and covered with lumps. Instead of a head, there were twelve long arms coming out of its neck. On every arm were twelve winking eyes.

For one second, Dad stood still, with his mouth wide open.

The eyes glared at him, and the arms reached out towards him.

Dad took three paces backwards. "Run, Kristy!" he shouted. "Run for your life!"

Then Dad ran as fast as he could, back along the path. It wasn't until he reached the front garden that he realised Kristy wasn't with him. He skidded to a halt.

CHAPTER 2

How Many Aliens?

"Kristy?" called Dad.

There was no answer from Kristy. Instead, he heard a wailing noise coming from inside the house.

It was Kristy's little brother, Jamie.

"Wa-a-a-ah! I saw an alien! Wa-a-a-a-a-ah!"

Dad rushed in through the front door, and down the hall to the kitchen. Jamie was sitting on the floor beside the fridge. Wet bubbles hung from his nose.

Dad picked him up and patted him on the back. "What's the matter Jamie? What is it?"

"In the bushes! Down the back! Alien!"

"There, there." Dad patted him again. "I saw it too. Yellow with long arms."

"No-o-o!" yelled Jamie. "It was brown and hairy!"

"Brown?" Dad frowned. "Hairy?"

"Kristy took me to see it! It was horrible! Wa-a-a-ah!"

Dad put Jamie back down on the floor. Now he was really puzzled.

Dad went into the back garden. There was no sign of Kristy. He crossed the lawn and peered into the bushy area. Where was the yellow creature?

Dad tiptoed down the path, one step at a time. Then he saw it.

The yellow creature had shrunk to a quarter of its size. It was wobbly and its arms hung down. Even as Dad watched, the creature grew smaller and smaller. Now it looked blurry around the edges.

"Where am I?" croaked a feeble voice.

For a moment, Dad thought it was the alien. Then he saw a pair of legs sticking out from under the bushes. The legs were wearing fluffy blue slippers.

It could only be Auntie Veetie! Dad hurried to help.

Auntie Veetie sat up suddenly, looking dizzy. Her glasses had slipped sideways. "Who's that?" she gasped.

"Only me," said Dad.

"George? Oh, thank goodness. I must have fainted. I saw something dreadful, George."

"Hah! Something like an alien?"

"Yes!" said Auntie Veetie. "A shiny purple thing. It was reaching out for us with a long red tongue."

"Us?" asked Dad.

"Kristy and me. Where is she? George, you have to take care of the children."

Dad looked cross. "I'll take care of her all right. *Kristy!*" he shouted.

Dad stared at the yellow creature. Then Auntie Veetie saw it too. She took one look, and fainted again.

CHAPTER 3

Kristy's Black Box

"*Kristy!*" bellowed Dad.

There was a loud click and the alien vanished. One minute it was there, the next minute it was gone.

Dad spotted Kristy hiding in the bushes. He dragged her out onto the path.

"Ow-ow!" she yelled.

Kristy tried to get away, but it was no use. Dad turned her around to face him. She was holding a large black box.

"So!" shouted Dad. "It *was* you! It was all a trick!"

"I was only practising," said Kristy in a small voice.

"What do you mean, practising?" said Dad.

"I was practising my acting," she said. "I was pretending I'd seen an alien."

Dad stared at Kristy. "You scare people half to death and say it's *acting*?" he said.

"Did I scare *you* half to death?" asked Kristy.

Dad didn't answer the question. "Jamie was terrified," he said. "Auntie Veetie fainted."

Kristy grinned suddenly. "I must be good then! I had you all believing. I reckon I could be a megastar!"

Dad looked at the black box in Kristy's arms. "What are you carrying there?" he asked.

"This?" said Kristy. "My projector. It shows pictures of aliens."

"Where *do* you get these things?" Dad snorted. "You can start by saying sorry to Auntie Veetie."

Kristy put the box on the ground beside the path. She went and stood in front of Auntie Veetie's fluffy blue slippers.

"Sorry, Auntie Veetie," Kristy said.

There was no answer. Auntie Veetie hadn't yet woken up from her second faint.

"Now say sorry to Jamie," said Dad.

He pushed Kristy towards the house. Jamie was still blubbering in the kitchen. Kristy stuck out her tongue at him.

"Sorry, Jamie," she said sweetly.

Dad pointed the way to her bedroom door.

"And for punishment, you can stay in your room till dinner time."

"Aw, Dad," said Kristy. "Can't I just say sorry to you too?"

"No," said Dad.

Kristy pulled a face and went off. Dad waited to see the door close behind her. Then he marched out into the back garden again. He wanted to take another look at the black box that Kristy had called her projector. The more he thought about it, the more of a mystery it seemed.

But when he got there, it had gone.

CHAPTER 4
Reality TV?

Two hours later, Kristy was still in her bedroom. She had brushed her hair and put on her smartest top, white with gold glitter. She was practising her acting in front of the mirror. Then came a tap on the window.

"Is that you, Meggethor?" said Kristy.

"It is," replied a strange, deep voice.

Kristy went across and opened the window. Meggethor slid in and stood – if you can call it standing – in the middle of the floor.

He was one metre tall and one metre wide. His mouth and ears were like trumpets. He had only one eye, with a furry eyebrow all around.

"Is three enough?" Kristy asked.

"Thr-r-ee is excellent," answered Meggethor. His trumpet-mouth found the 'r' hard to say.

He carried lots of things used in filming, including lights and a camera. He also had Kristy's projector.

Meggethor began to set the things up around the bedroom.

"Do I stand or sit?" asked Kristy.

"Sit." Meggethor pointed to the bed with his trumpet-mouth.

Kristy sat down on the side of the bed. Meggethor pointed with his trumpet-mouth to a small screen on his chest.

"You r-r-read your scr-r-r-ipt from this scr-r-r-reen."

He raised the camera to his eye. The camera began to hum.

Kristy read as the words moved slowly up the screen.

"*Hi there, Galacticans! The next part of our show tonight comes to you from planet Earth. I'm Kristy O'Connell. Welcome!*"

She smiled into the camera.

"*Tonight, our three Earthlings are introduced to three types of Galacticans. An Altivarian from the planet Org, a Dronkite from the planet D'lash, and a Plinnikon from the planet Plinnikut. A special hi to all you Altivarians, Dronkites and Plinnikons!*

"*Remember, no Earthling has ever met another Galactic species before. You'll see shock, horror, weeping – and even fainting! So make yourselves comfortable, sit back and enjoy the fun!*"

The screen went blank. Meggethor nodded and lowered his camera.

"You'r-r-re a knock-out," he told her.

Kristy grinned. "Did you say eighty-five billion Galacticans will be watching?"

"That's r-r-right. They love this stuff. It's the reality TV hit of the year."

"Galacticans must have a weird sense of humour," said Kristy.

Meggethor raised his camera again. "Are you r-r-ready for your closing lines?"

Kristy nodded, and read the new words appearing on the screen.

"That was the exciting world of planet Earth – getting its first introduction to the rest of the Galaxy! And now, it's goodbye from me, Kristy O'Connell. Stay tuned to see what's going on out there on the planet Hunx."